Plight of the Wild Geese

In 1689 James Stuart, King of England, Ireland, and Scotland, was deposed by William of Orange in an event known as the Glorious Revolution. James fled to his cousin in France, Louis XIV, the most powerful monarch in Europe. Louis was at war with William of Orange, who formed a league, known as the Grand Alliance after the inclusion of England, opposed to Louis' aggressive expansionist policies. Louis saw James as a means by which he could keep William III preoccupied, while he fought his enemies in Europe. As such, James was sent to Ireland with arms and supplies in a bid to reclaim his throne.

During his reign James had sent Richard Talbot, Earl of Tyrconnell, to Ireland as Lord Deputy. Tyrconnell placed Catholics in positions of control, purged the army of Protestants, and raised an Irish Catholic army for James. Since the Cromwellian Settlement Irish Catholic lands had been confiscated in order to pay the soldiers and creditors of Cromwell's New Model Army, who repressed the Confederate Wars of 1641-1652 in Ireland. This act also prohibited Catholics from holding public offices or bearing arms. No Catholic could vote, or so much as carry a sword. Therefore, when news of James' expected arrival reached Ireland the Catholics of the country began to raise their heads as the promise of liberty, and prosperity appeared to lie once again under the banner of a Stuart.

James Stuart landed at Kinsale on 12th March 1689, and proceeded to lead a ruinous campaign against the Williamites. After a series of disasters, culminating in the Battle of the Boyne, James fled to France, leaving the Irish to continue the fight against William's forces in Ireland. Divisions plagued the Jacobite army, who successfully repulsed the Williamite Siege of Limerick in 1690. After this event William of Orange departed Ireland leaving General de Ginkel in command of his forces in Ireland. Both sides went into winter quarters and began to prepare for the campaign the following year.

Tyrconnell had lost faith in the Jacobite cause after the Battle of the Boyne, but his faith was restored by the successful defence of Limerick against William's army. He decides to go to France in order to appeal to Louis XIV for further aid in order to continue the war in Ireland.

moccupress
www.moccupress.com

DECEMBER 1690, TYRCONNELL ARRIVES AT LOUIS XIV'S PALACE AT VERSAILLES, FRANCE.

I IMPLORE HIS MOST CHRISTIAN MAJESTY TO PROVIDE SUPPLIES, TROOPS, & AN ABLE GENERAL TO LEAD KING JAMES' ARMY IN IRELAND AGAINST OUR COMMON ENEMY.

I'M WILLING TO GRANT FURTHER ASSISTANCE, SOLELY BECAUSE THE MOUNTCASHEL BRIGADE HAS DONE WONDERS FOR MY CAMPAIGN IN ITALY...

4

Plight of the Wild Geese

Script by Dermot Poyntz

❊

Artwork by Lee Grace

moccupress
www.moccupress.com

———◦◦◦———

To the memory of the Irish Brigade (1690-1792)

Oh! Patrick Sarsfield, Ireland's wonder, Who fought in field like any thunder,
One of King James' chief commanders, Now lies the food of crows in Flanders!
Och hone, Och hone.

Published by Moccu Press, 2011
Email: moccupress@yahoo.com
Website: www.moccupress.com

ISBN: 978-0-956655844

Printed by New Pearl River Printing, Guangzhou City, China.

———◦◦◦———

"...HAVING ARRIVED IN FRANCE DURING THE SUMMER OF 1690, THESE IRISH TROOPS WERE QUICKLY FORMED INTO A BRIGADE..."

KING LOUIS CALLS UPON YOU TO GO TO THE FRONT WHERE YOU ARE URGENTLY NEEDED.

"...AND SO 5,000 MEN UNDER MOUNTCASHELL MARCHED TOWARDS THE ITALIAN FRONTIER TO SUPPORT MY ARMY THERE..."

6

7

MAY 1691, ST RUTH REACHES LIMERICK.

ALLOW ME TO INTRODUCE TWO OF MY FINEST OFFICERS, LIEUTENANT-GENERAL DE TESSE & GENERAL D'USSON.

IRELAND WELCOMES YOUR ARRIVAL.

ORANGE HAS LEFT GENERAL DE GINKEL IN COMMAND OF HIS FORCES IN IRELAND.

18,000 WILLIAMITES ARE MARCHING TOWARDS ATHLONE, TO FORCE A PASSAGE OVER THE SHANNON.

CAMP THE ENTIRE JACOBITE ARMY TWO MILES SOUTH OF ATHLONE. D'USSON WILL COMMAND THE TOWN'S GARRISON.

Athlone

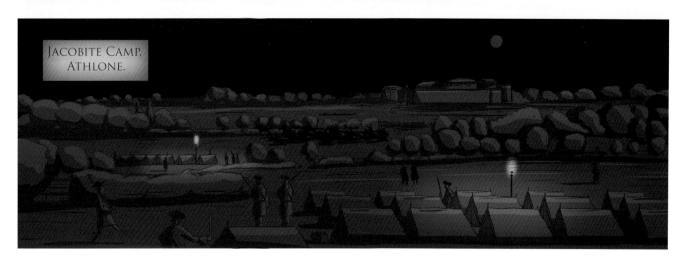
JACOBITE CAMP, ATHLONE.

LAST YEAR ATHLONE WAS SUCCESSFULLY DEFENDED BY A WALL BUILT ON THE SOUTH SIDE OF THE TOWN, FACING OUR CAMP...

...THIS STRUCTURE IS NOW AN OBSTACLE TO THE SENDING OF REINFORCEMENTS INTO ATHLONE. I STRONGLY ADVISE THAT IT BE PULLED DOWN.

OUR AIM IS TO HOLD DEFENSIVE POSITIONS, NOT TEAR THEM DOWN!

DON'T INTERFERE IN MILITARY MATTERS OF WHICH YOU KNOW NOTHING!

MY LORD, SOME OF THE IRISH COLONELS INSIST THAT UNLESS YOU QUIT THE CAMP, THEY'LL CUT THE CORDS OF YOUR TENT.

TREACHEROUS SCOUNDRELS!

CRASHHh

TYRCONNELL DEPARTS FOR LIMERICK.

MORE THAN HALF THE ARMY IS LOYAL TO ME! I WON'T BE HELD RESPONSIBLE FOR DIVISIONS ON THE EVE OF A DECISIVE BATTLE

JUNE 19, 1691, GENERAL DE GINKEL SURVEYS ATHLONE.

THE TOWN IS DIVIDED BY THE RIVER SHANNON. ENGLISH TOWN OCCUPIES THE EAST BANK, IRISH TOWN THE WEST...

...BOTH SIDES ARE CONNECTED BY A SINGLE BRIDGE.

ENGLISH TOWN IS SURROUNDED BY STONE WALLS, BUT IRISH TOWN IS LIGHTLY PROTECTED. THE RIVER IS GUARDED BY ATHLONE CASTLE, ON THE WEST SIDE.

THE JACOBITES PLAN THEIR DEFENSE.

WE`LL DEFEND ENGLISH TOWN, & FORCE THE WILLIAMITES TO EXHAUST THEMSELVES THROUGH COSTLY ASSAULTS. IF ENGLISH TOWN IS OVERRUN THE GARRISON WILL FALL BACK TO IRISH TOWN, & DESTROY THE BRIDGE BEHIND THEM.

KABOOM

KABOOM

KABOOM

THE WILLIAMITES SOON OPEN A BREACH INTO ENGLISH TOWN. THE ARTILLERY CONTINUES TO FIRE, PREVENTING THE DEFENDERS FROM MAKING REPAIRS.

By nightfall de Ginkel holds English Town.

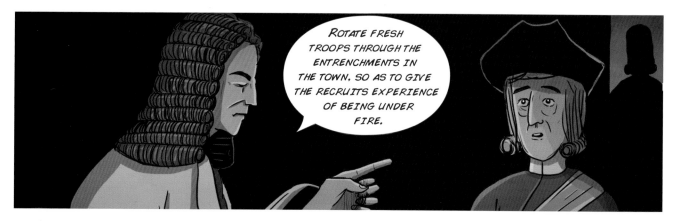

THE CANNONBALLS AND BOMBS FLY SO THICK, THAT IRISH TOWN BECOMES HELL ON EARTH

DE GINKEL'S MEN ATTEMPT TO REPAIR THE BRIDGE UNDER COVER OF DARKNESS.

WE HAVE TO STOP THEM. I NEED VOLUNTEERS!

WILLIAMITE SHARPSHOOTERS!

CRACK

CRACK

CRACK

AHHH!

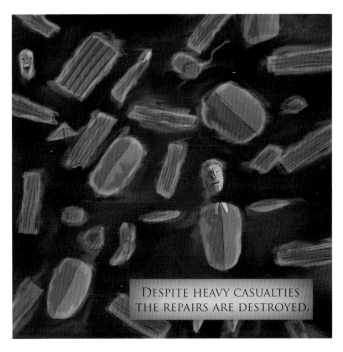

DESPITE HEAVY CASUALTIES THE REPAIRS ARE DESTROYED.

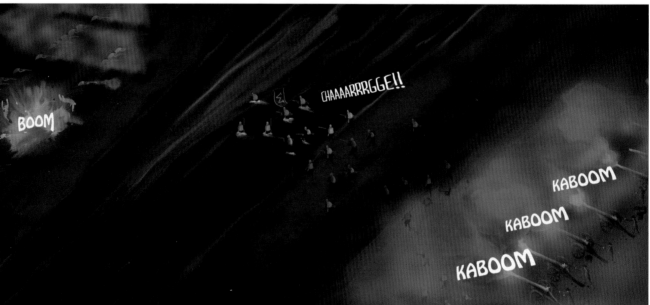

17

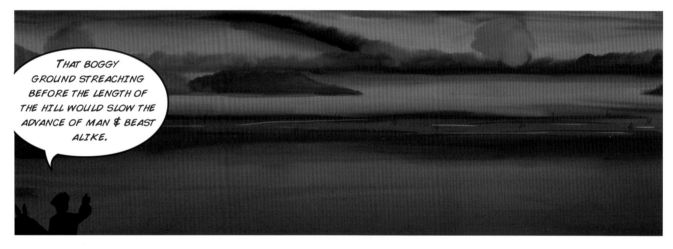

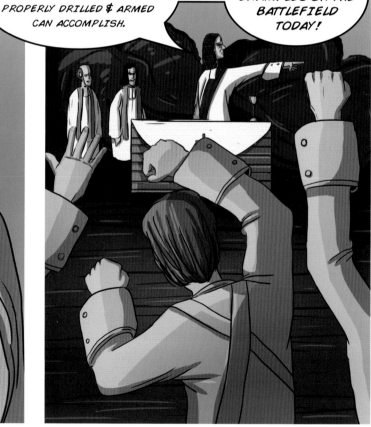

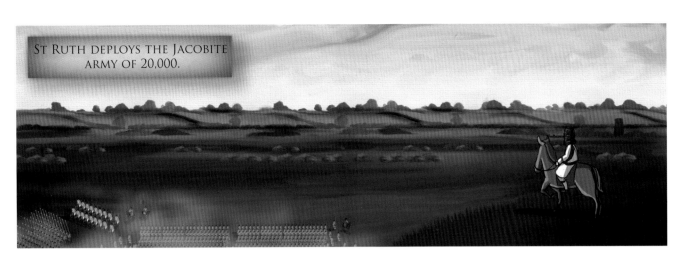

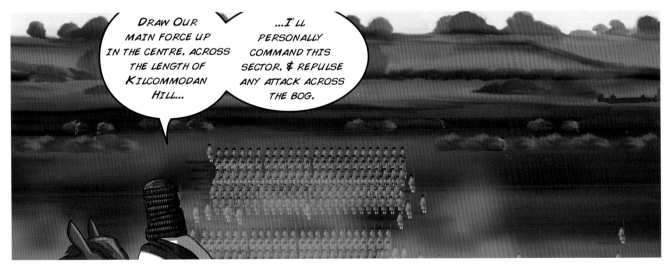

23

THE WILLIAMITE DRAGOONS ADVANCE TOWARDS THE BRIDGE.

CRACK CRACK CRACK CRACK

DE GINKEL SENDS REINFORCEMENTS.

SARSFIELD ALSO COMMITS SUPPORT.

THE GRIZZLY CONTEST FOR THE BRIDGE BECOMES A STALEMATE.

CRACK

SEND AN ENTIRE REGIMENT FORWARD, TO OVERWHELM THE ENEMY!

ST RUTH HAS MOVED A NUMBER OF INFANTRY UNITS TO HELP DEFEND THE ATTIBRASSIL BRIDGE.

LAUNCH ANOTHER ATTACK AT THIS POINT TO MAINTAIN PRESSURE...

...HE'LL CONTINUE TO WEAKEN THE REST OF THE JACOBITE LINE TO SUPPORT THE THREATENED FLANK.

WHILE THE BATTLE FOR THE BRIDGE RAGES, ATTACKS CAN BE LAUNCHED ALONG THEIR CENTRE.

DE GINKELL COMMANDS A MIXED DIVISION OF 3,000 TO ASSAULT THE ATTIBRASSIL BRIDGE.

THE WILLIAMITES HAVE COMMITTED TO OUR RIGHT FLANK...

...REPOSITION TROOPS TO SUPPORT THAT SECTOR.

DE GINKELS ARTILLERY ALSO CREEPS FORWARD.

29

MACKAY'S ARMY REACHES FIRM GROUND...

...WHERE THEY'RE MET WITH A VOLLEY OF JACOBITE MUSKETFIRE.

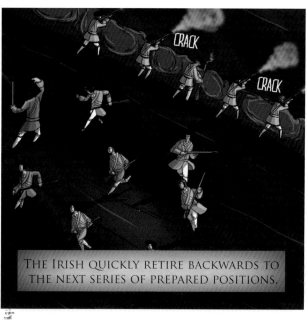

THE IRISH QUICKLY RETIRE BACKWARDS TO THE NEXT SERIES OF PREPARED POSITIONS.

MACKAY'S TROOPS ATTACK THE HEDGELINES ONLY TO FIND THEM EMPTY.

THIS TACTIC IS REPEATED, DRAWING THE WILLIAMITES UPSLOPE.

2,000 OF KING JAMES' FOOT GUARDS, LED BY THEIR CHAPLAIN, ADVANCE.

CHAAAAARGE!

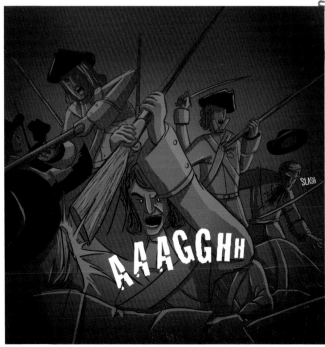

SLASH

AAAGGHH

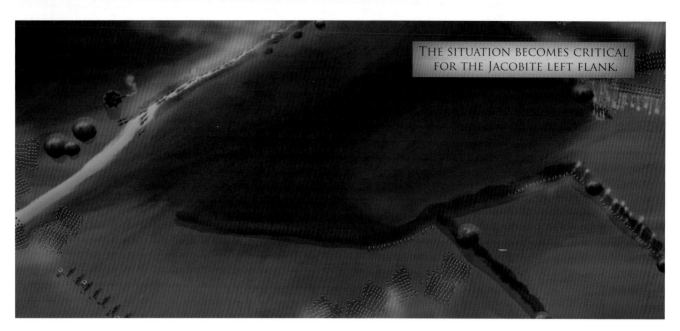

THE SITUATION BECOMES CRITICAL FOR THE JACOBITE LEFT FLANK.

CHAAARGE!!

LUTTRELL HAS QUIT THE FIELD!

ALL IS LOST!

SHELDON ALSO DESERTS HIS POST, TAKING THE ENTIRE JACOBITE LEFT FLANK WITH HIM.

THE WILLIAMITE CAVALRY ASCEND ONTO THE NORTHERN SLOPES OF KILCOMMODAN HILL.

THE JACOBITE CENTRE IS TAKEN BY COMPLETE SURPRISE.

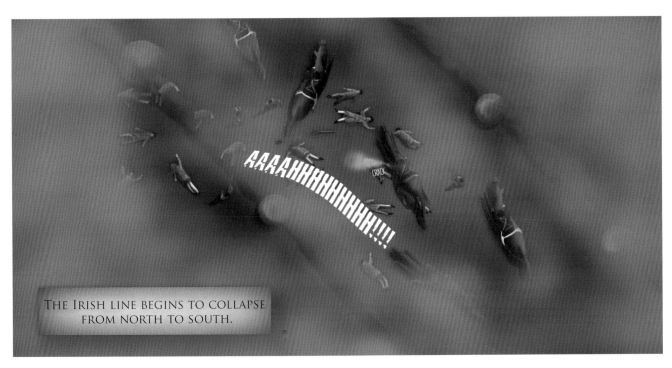

THE IRISH LINE BEGINS TO COLLAPSE FROM NORTH TO SOUTH.

36

COMMAND OF THE JACOBITE ARMY NOW FALLS TO SARSFIELD.

THE BATTLE IS LOST. ALL I CAN HOPE TO DO IS SAVE AS MANY MEN AS POSSIBLE.

SARSFIELD ORDERS THE JACOBITE RIGHT WING, A FORCE OF 2,500, TO DISENGAGE AND COVER THE RETREAT TOWARDS LIMERICK.

THE REMAINS OF THE JACOBITE ARMY REACHES LIMERICK.

WE'RE UTTERLY RUINED.

A FRENCH FLEET IS ON ITS WAY TO RELIEVE LIMERICK. WE'LL DEFEND THE CITY UNTIL THEY ARRIVE.

MEANWHILE, GALWAY SURRENDERS.

A FUTILE RESISTANCE WOULD'VE PROVOKED THE MASSACRE OF THE GARRISON...

...AN HONOURABLE SURRENDER ALLOWED US TO JOIN THE FINAL RALLY.

D'USSON ARRIVES IN LIMERICK WITH THE GALWAY GARRISON.

39

DE GINKEL'S ARMY SURROUNDS LIMERICK.

BOOM

AN ENGLISH NAVAL SQUADRON ARRIVES TO CONTEST THE RELIEF OF THE CITY.

TIME IS RUNNING OUT. I NEED TO FORCE LIMERICK INTO SURRENDER, & END THE WAR IN IRELAND BEFORE WINTER...

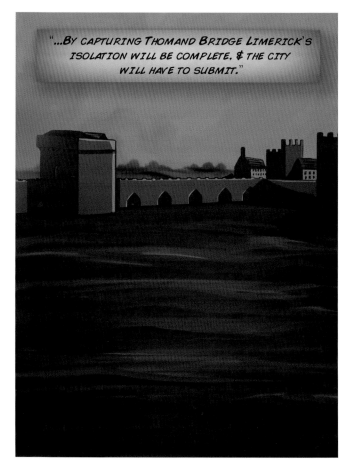

"...BY CAPTURING THOMAND BRIDGE LIMERICK'S ISOLATION WILL BE COMPLETE, & THE CITY WILL HAVE TO SUBMIT."

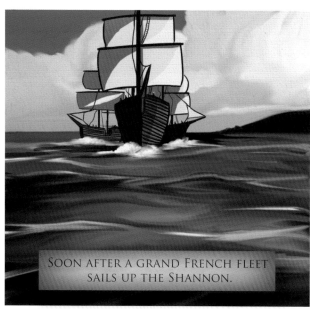

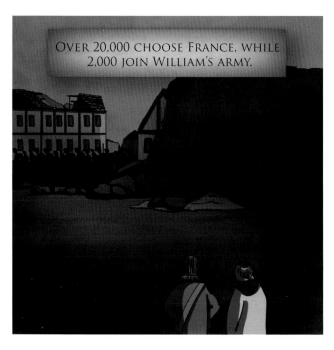

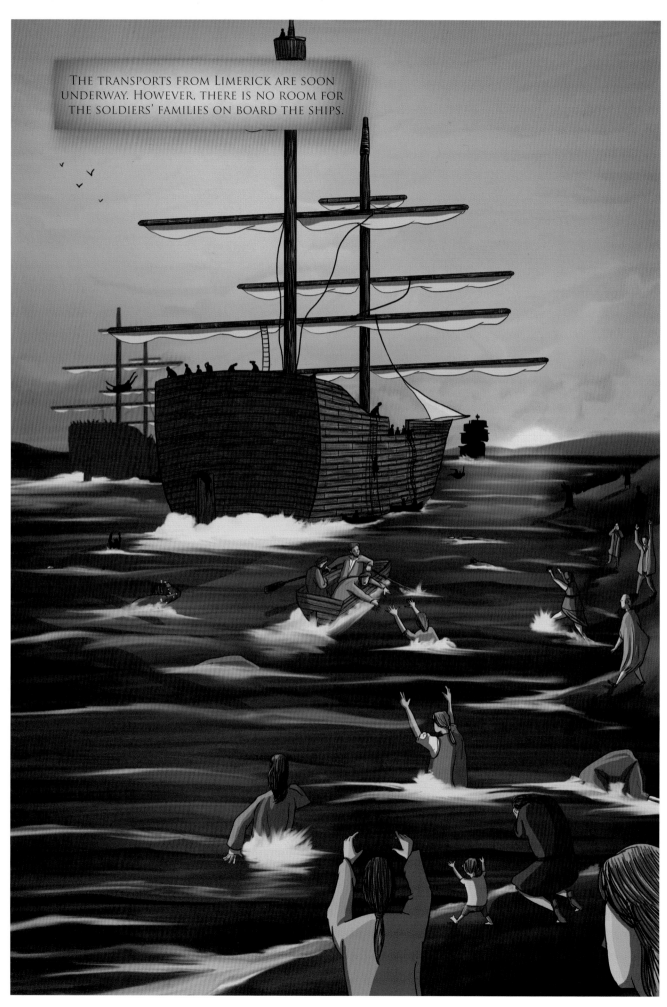

THE TRANSPORTS FROM LIMERICK ARE SOON UNDERWAY. HOWEVER, THERE IS NO ROOM FOR THE SOLDIERS' FAMILIES ON BOARD THE SHIPS.

KING JAMES INSPECTS THE IRISH EXILES ARRIVING IN FRANCE.

THIS FORCE IS MINE TO COMMAND AS I SEE FIT.

PROVIDENCE HAS FURNISHED ME WITH THE MEANS TO MAKE ONE MORE BID FOR MY LOST CROWN.

SO. YOU INTEND TO INVADE ENGLAND.

IT WOULD BE THE QUICKET WAY TO END WAR WITH THE LEAGUE...

...I'LL DO EVERYTHING I CAN TO ENSURE YOUR SUCCESS.

ALL THAT REMAINS IS TO GET MY ARMY OVER THE OCEAN INTO ENGLAND.

APRIL 1692, JAMES WAITS TO CROSS THE ENGLISH CHANNEL WITH A FORCE OF 20,000.

THE COMBINED ANGLO-DUTCH FLEET OF OVER 80 SHIPS LIES IN WAIT AT SPITHEAD.

ADMIRAL TOURVILLE, FRANCE'S MOST ABLE SAILOR, IS TASKED TO CLEAR THE CHANNEL.

TOURVILLE ENTERS THE CHANNEL WITH HIS FORTY-FOUR SHIPS OF THE LINE.

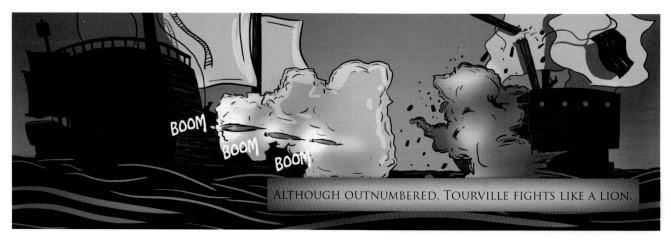

BOOM
BOOM
BOOM

ALTHOUGH OUTNUMBERED, TOURVILLE FIGHTS LIKE A LION.

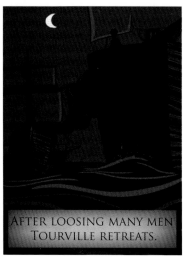

AFTER LOOSING MANY MEN TOURVILLE RETREATS.

FRANCE HAS LOST ITS NAVAL EQUALITY, ALONG WITH ANY CHANCE OF EVER INVADING ENGLAND...

...JAMES' IRISH TROOPS CAN FINALLY BE DEPLOYED AGAINST MY FOES ON THE CONTINENT...

...SADLY JAMES HIMSELF HAS BECOME DETACHED FROM REALITY, & SPENDS MOST OF HIS TIME ALONE AT PRAYER.

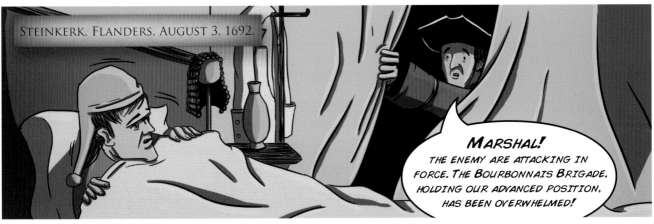

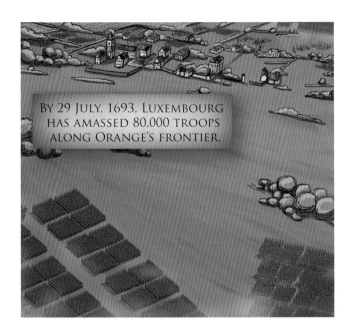

By 29 July, 1693, Luxembourg has amassed 80,000 troops along Orange's frontier.

William's line is held by a force of 50,000.

The village of Landen in Belgium is the key to King William's entire position.

Throughout the battle for Landen the village changes hands again and again.

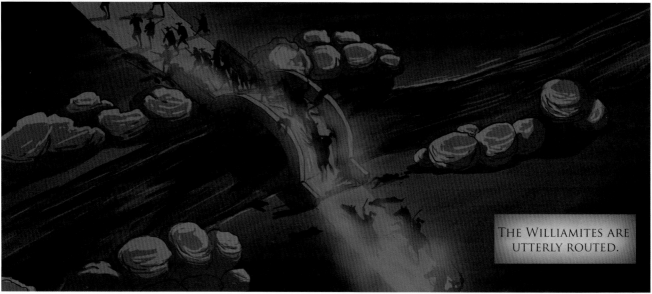

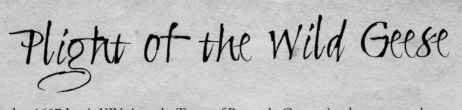

Plight of the Wild Geese

On 20 September 1697 Louis XIV signs the Treaty of Ryswyck. Orange is reluctant to make peace, but realises that it's as necessary for the Dutch Republic as it is for France. The main consequence of the treaty is Louis' recognition of William as King of England. James Stuart's hopes of reclaiming his throne are shattered. Louis makes peace for financial reasons. As such, the first measure he takes after peace is declared is the reduction of his armies. By January 1698, the French army of 250,000 is reduced to 150, 000. For the French soldiers it's a blessing. Their fields need tillage, and their vineyards call for attention. For the Irish exiles in France the reduction of the army proves to be anything but a blessing. They cannot return to Ireland.

12,000 Irish soldiers are suddenly deprived of their only livelihood. In Ireland there had been no opportunity to follow the pursuits of an ordinary life. They have no qualifications, they know no trade, have no industry, and are skilful at nothing. One thing alone they had mastered, the profession of the soldier. Many receive shelter at the old palace of St. Germains, which soon becomes full of Irish beggars.

The situation is aggravated by the arrival of the Irish expelled from Ireland under the Penal Laws, which determine to root out of Popery and banish all priests, who also come flocking over into France. These laws break the terms of the Treaty of Limerick. During France's four years' peace the ranks of the Irish Brigade are decimated by extreme poverty, until the reconstruction of the Irish Brigade in 1701.

The departure of the majority of the survivors of James' Irish army leaves those who remained in Ireland entirely at the mercy of the Penal Laws. The Irish Catholic peasantry, for a century after the Treaty of Limerick, are reduced to the lowest state of serfdom verging on savagery.

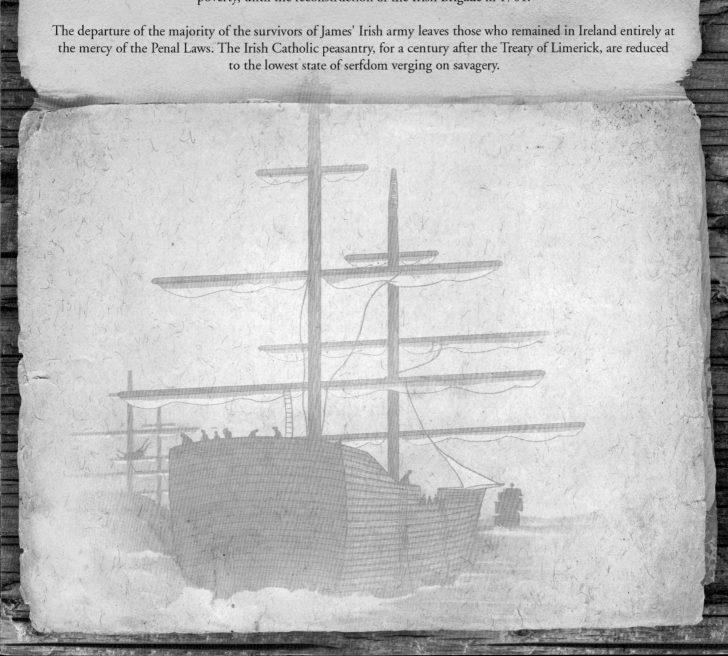